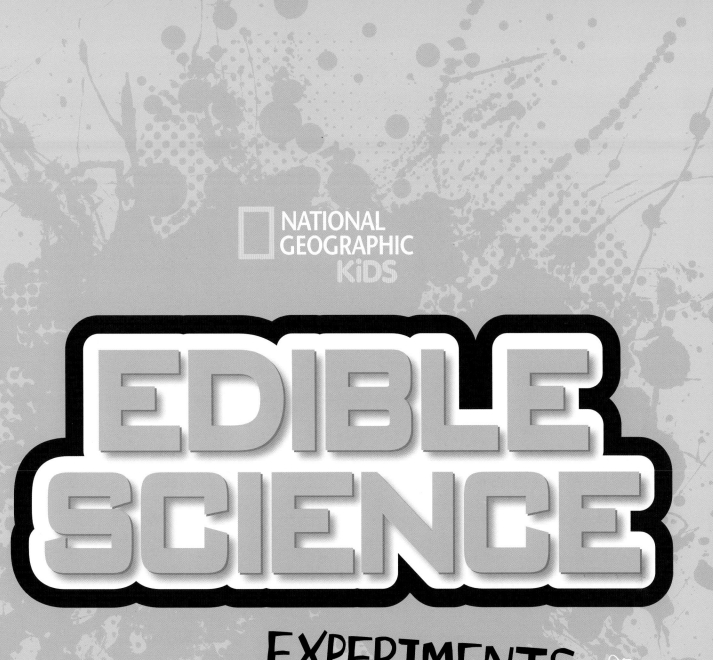

NATIONAL
GEOGRAPHIC
KiDS

EDIBLE SCIENCE

EXPERIMENTS YOU CAN EAT

JODI WHEELER-TOPPEN
WITH CAROL TENNANT

NATIONAL GEOGRAPHIC
WASHINGTON, D.C.

Staff for this Book
Erica Green, *Project Editor*
Amanda Larsen, *Art Director*
Lori Epstein, *Photo Editor*
Paige Towler, *Editorial Assistant*
Sanjida Rashid, *Design Production Assistant*
Colm McKeveny, *Rights Clearance Specialist*
Michael Cassady, *Rights Clearance Assistant*
Grace Hill, *Managing Editor*
Mike O'Connor, *Production Editor*
Susan Borke, *Legal and Business Affairs*

Published by the National Geographic Society
Gary E. Knell, *President and CEO*
John M. Fahey, *Chairman of the Board*
Melina Gerosa Bellows, *Chief Education Officer*
Declan Moore, *Chief Media Officer*
Hector Sierra, *Senior Vice President and General Manager, Book Division*

Senior Management Team, Kids Publishing and Media
Nancy Laties Feresten, *Senior Vice President;* Jennifer Emmett, *Vice President, Editorial Director, Kids Books;* Julie Vosburgh Agnone, *Vice President, Editorial Operations;* Rachel Buchholz, *Editor and Vice President,* NG Kids *magazine;* Michelle Sullivan, *Vice President, Kids Digital;* Eva Absher-Schantz, *Design Director;* Jay Sumner, *Photo Director;* Hannah August, *Marketing Director;* R. Gary Colbert, *Production Director*

Digital Anne McCormack, *Director;* Laura Goertzel, Sara Zeglin, *Producers;* Jed Winer, *Special Projects Assistant;* Emma Rigney, *Creative Producer;* Brian Ford, *Video Producer;* Bianca Bowman, *Assistant Producer;* Natalie Jones, *Senior Product Manager*

Created and Produced by Ivy Kids
Kim Hankinson, *Art Director*
Judith Chamberlain-Webber, *Project Editor*
Ginny Zeal, *Designer*
Carol Tennant, *Recipe Text*
Susanna Tee, *Food Stylist*
Rachel Fuller, *Illustration*
Emma Wood, *Photography*

 The National Geographic Society is one of the world's largest nonprofit scientific and educational organizations. Founded in 1888 to "increase and diffuse geographic knowledge," the Society's mission is to inspire people to care about the planet. It reaches more than 400 million people worldwide each month through its official journal, *National Geographic,* and other magazines; National Geographic Channel; television documentaries; music; radio; films; books; DVDs; maps; exhibitions; live events; school publishing programs; interactive media; and merchandise. National Geographic has funded more than 10,000 scientific research, conservation, and exploration projects and supports an education program promoting geographic literacy.

For more information, please visit nationalgeographic.com, call 1-800-NGS LINE (647-5463), or write to the following address:
National Geographic Society
1145 17th Street N.W.
Washington, D.C. 20036-4688 U.S.A.

Visit us online at nationalgeographic.com/books

For librarians and teachers: ngchildrensbooks.org

More for kids from National Geographic:
kids.nationalgeographic.com

For information about special discounts for bulk purchases, please contact National Geographic Books Special Sales: ngspecsales@ngs.org

For rights or permissions inquiries, please contact National Geographic Books Subsidiary Rights: ngbookrights@ngs.org

Trade paperback ISBN: 978-1-4263-2111-5
Reinforced library edition ISBN: 978-1-4263-2112-2

Printed in China
15/IVY/1

CONTENTS

INTRODUCTION

Did you know that your kitchen is also a science lab? Every time you cook, you are doing a science experiment. In this book, we'll explore the science of food right in your very own kitchen science lab. And the best part is, almost all the experiments will be edible!

To understand the science of cooking, we have to examine the most basic components of food. Take a scoop of ice cream, for example. It may seem like one solid chunk, but, as with everything else around you, it is made up of tiny particles called atoms. These atoms can be joined together in groups called molecules. Most foods contain a variety of molecules. That ice cream, for example, contains molecules of fat, sugar, water, protein, and other chemicals.

Chemicals! In ice cream? About that word "chemicals" ... Scientifically, a chemical is a substance with a set molecular arrangement. For instance, water is always made of two hydrogen atoms joined to an oxygen atom, meaning water is a chemical. So while it may sound strange to talk about eating chemicals, it's a scientifically accurate description. And as you'll see, what happens when we cook depends on the chemical nature of the ingredients we choose.

With that said, grab your chef's hat and your chemist's goggles, and let's dig into the science of food!

BE SAFE! While you work through the experiments in this book, keep a few safety rules in mind. Have an adult help with sharp knives, the oven, and the stove top. Be careful when you touch things that have come out of the oven—remember that hot pans and cold pans look the same. And finally, though most of these experiments are intended to be eaten, there are a few that you shouldn't actually eat. Watch for those. Although none of them are poisonous, they might not feel very good in your stomach.

CHAPTER ONE

MIXING AND UNMIXING

>> When cooks combine ingredients, they call it a mixture. Scientists use the same word to describe a combination of substances that keep their chemical structure after being mixed. In this section, we'll look at how things mix together and how to separate them.

ICE CREAM
IN A BAG

STOPPING SEPARATION

> Active time needed
> **20 minutes**

Milk is a complicated mixture of lots of different kinds of molecules, including fats, proteins, and water. Normally, freezing would cause milk to separate into its various parts. The trick to making ice cream is to get the cream cold enough to freeze without the parts separating. The success of this recipe comes down to keeping things moving. Get ready to squish, shimmy, and shake your way to dessert!

YOU NEED

SUPPLIES
2 qt.-size ziplock bags, 1 gal.-size ziplock bag, dish towel

INGREDIENTS
¼ cup heavy cream
¼ cup whole milk
½ tsp. vanilla extract
1 Tbsp. sugar
4 cups crushed ice
4 Tbsp. rock salt

WATCH FOR IT!
Open up the bag, and you'll have ice cream.

> MOLECULE: a group of connected atoms

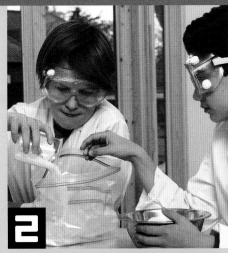

KEEP IT MOVING!

INSTRUCTIONS

1 Put the cream, milk, vanilla, and sugar in one qt.-size ziplock bag. Remove as much air as possible and seal the bag well. Put this bag inside the second qt.-size bag, again removing as much air as possible and sealing it well. (Double-bagging the ice cream mixture will help to prevent leakage.)

2 Put the double-bagged mixture into the gal.-size ziplock bag and add the ice and salt. Once again, remove as much air as possible from the bag and seal it well.

3 Wrap the bag in the dish towel. Shake and massage the bag, ensuring that the inner bag is surrounded by the ice. Keep massaging it for 5–8 minutes.

4 Open the bag. Inside, the mixture will have frozen into ice cream!

THE SCIENCE SCOOP

When water molecules freeze, they line up in a neat, orderly, and tight formation, so there's not much room for other molecules to mix in. If you just put your ingredients in the freezer, the water molecules would separate out as large chunks of ice. But when you toss and shake the molecules in the bag, they can't connect or easily get a grip on one another. Only microscopic chunks of ice are able to form, keeping the water mixed in with everything else. It's hard for water to freeze when there are other molecules in the way, so the temperature has to be colder than that for making regular ice for it to happen. That's where your outer bag of ice and salt comes in. Salt lowers the temperature of the ice so that your ice cream mix is cold enough to freeze.

SEMI-ORDERED WATER MOLECULES

ORDERED ICE MOLECULES

ORANGE VINAIGRETTE

SOME THINGS WON'T MIX

You shake up your bottle of salad dressing and pour it on your greens. But by the time you pass it to your sister, you can already see a layer of oil gathering on top. The dressing won't stay mixed. To understand why certain liquids won't stay blended, we have to look at the individual molecules in these ingredients. Let's make this vinaigrette to find out what's going on between the oil and vinegar in dressing.

KEEP IT MOVING!

YOU NEED

SUPPLIES
Measuring spoons, grater, small bowl, whisk

INGREDIENTS
3 Tbsp. extra-virgin olive oil
2 Tbsp. orange juice
2 tsp. cider vinegar
1 tsp. finely grated orange zest
Salt and freshly ground pepper to taste
Rainbow Salad (opposite) or other favorite
 salad

INSTRUCTIONS

1 In a small bowl, whisk together the oil, orange juice, vinegar, orange zest, and salt and pepper. Use immediately to dress your salad.

THE SCIENCE SCOOP

If you could peer inside an atom, you would see that it is made of even smaller pieces. One smaller piece is called an electron, and electrons are what make electricity. Vinegar and orange juice are made mostly of water molecules. The electrons in a water molecule hang out on one side of the molecule more than the other. This gives water molecules an uneven electrical charge. One side of the molecule is a tiny bit negative. The other side is a tiny bit positive. The negative side of one water molecule tends to stick to the positive side of another. Oil molecules don't have positive and negative sides, so they get left out when the water molecules arrange themselves. To get a good mixture of oil and water on your salad, you have to shake them up and pour them before they can separate.

LET'S WATCH HOW PLANTS GET WATER

BONUS: RAINBOW SALAD

Lettuce has a built-in system for moving water around. In this activity, you'll move colored water through the lettuce. When you're done, you'll be able to see the path that water takes through the leaf. You'll also have a fun, multicolored snack!

YOU NEED

TIME
4 hours

SUPPLIES
4 bowls

INGREDIENTS
Food coloring (minimum 4 colors)
Iceberg lettuce

INSTRUCTIONS

1 Fill the bowls with water. Make each bowl of water a different color by adding 10 drops of food coloring to each bowl.

2 Carefully tear the leaves from the head of lettuce. Immediately stick the leaves into each of the bowls of water, with the top of the leaf sticking out.

3 Let the lettuce sit for at least 4 hours.

WATCH FOR IT!
The lettuce leaves will turn the color of the food coloring. If you look closely, you'll see that the color is concentrated in connected lines throughout the leaf.

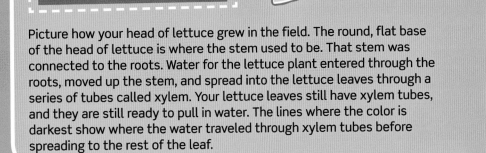

THE SCIENCE SCOOP

Picture how your head of lettuce grew in the field. The round, flat base of the head of lettuce is where the stem used to be. That stem was connected to the roots. Water for the lettuce plant entered through the roots, moved up the stem, and spread into the lettuce leaves through a series of tubes called xylem. Your lettuce leaves still have xylem tubes, and they are still ready to pull in water. The lines where the color is darkest show where the water traveled through xylem tubes before spreading to the rest of the leaf.

ORANGE MAYONNAISE

EMULSIFYING LIQUIDS

Difficulty level
Medium

Active time needed
20 minutes

WATCH FOR IT!
The oil and vinegar blend without separating.

You saw in Orange Vinaigrette (p. 8) that water and oil don't mix ... usually. Mayonnaise is the exception to this rule. Mayonnaise and vinaigrette have almost exactly the same ingredients, yet mayonnaise is creamy and does not separate into parts. Why is that? Try this recipe to find out. Here's a hint: The secret is in the eggs.

THE SCIENCE SCOOP

Remember that oil and water don't usually mix because their molecules are so different. However, egg yolks contain a group of molecules called emulsifiers. Emulsifiers have one end with a slight electrical charge that mixes well with water. The other end is not charged and mixes well with oil. So think of emulsifiers as go-betweens that can connect oil and water. Now who says oil and water can't mix?

YOU NEED

SUPPLIES
Measuring cup and spoons, bowl, grater, whisk

INGREDIENTS
2 pasteurized egg yolks (save the whites for something else, perhaps the Baked Alaska recipe, p. 21)
1–2 Tbsp. orange juice
Salt and freshly ground pepper
1 cup olive oil (not extra-virgin)
½ cup vegetable oil
2 tsp. finely grated orange zest
1–2 tsp. white wine vinegar

INSTRUCTIONS

1 In a bowl, whisk together the egg yolks and 1 Tbsp. of the orange juice, along with pinches of salt and pepper, until the yolks foam.

2 Drizzle the olive oil into the egg mixture in a slow, thin stream, whisking all the while.

3 Drizzle in the vegetable oil, adding it in a little faster, until all the oil is incorporated. Add the orange zest, and then whisk in 1 tsp. of vinegar. Adjust the flavor by adding the remaining 1 Tbsp. of orange juice and 1 tsp. of vinegar.

LET'S WATCH HOW EMULSIFIERS WORK

BONUS: DISAPPEARING GUM

Pop a piece of gum into your mouth and chew, chew, chew. No matter how hard you go at it, the gum is still there. Add a bit of chocolate, though, and the gum seems to disappear in your mouth. In this activity you'll see why candy companies don't make chocolate-covered gum.

WATCH FOR IT!
The gum dissolves in your mouth, and you end up swallowing it with the chocolate. Don't worry, all those stories of gum taking years to digest are false. It passes out of your system with other non-digestible waste.

YOU NEED

TIME
1 minute

SUPPLIES
Your mouth!

INGREDIENTS
1 piece chewing gum
1 piece chocolate

INSTRUCTIONS

1 Put the gum in your mouth and start chewing.

2 Put the piece of chocolate in your mouth and chew it with the gum.

3 Keep chewing. Notice something happening to the gum?

THE SCIENCE SCOOP

The first question you might ask is, Why doesn't gum dissolve every time you chew it (even without chocolate)? The answer is that, like oil, gum is made of molecules that don't mix well with water. Your saliva is mostly water, and since it can't mix into the gum, it doesn't start breaking the gum apart. Adding chocolate, though, has the same effect as adding an egg to oil and water. One of the molecules in chocolate is an emulsifier (remember, the connector) that can connect water to gum. Once a gum molecule is hooked to a saliva molecule, it can be carried off down your throat.

BLOCK O' BUTTER

SEPARATING SOLIDS AND LIQUIDS

Cow's milk is a complicated mixture of all the water, fats, proteins, sugars, vitamins, and minerals that a calf needs until it can eat on its own. Humans use it to make all kinds of foods, including butter, yogurt, custard, ice cream, and a variety of cheeses. Each of these foods involves separating milk in a different way. To begin exploring the mixture we call milk, you'll use this recipe to separate out the fat molecules inside milk in order to turn it into a clump of butter.

YOU NEED

SUPPLIES
2 qt.-size ziplock bags or a glass jar, measuring cups and spoons, baking parchment paper, paper towel

INGREDIENTS
2 cups heavy cream, at room temperature
Pinch of salt, plus more to taste

TIP
The butter forms faster if you start with the cream at room temperature.

1

3

> MEMBRANE: a thin covering

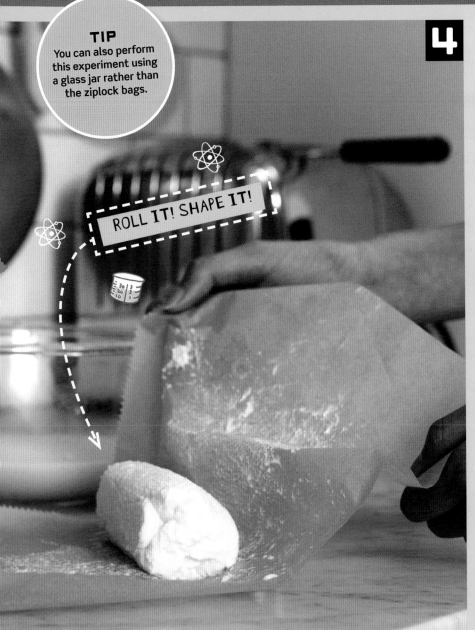

TIP
You can also perform this experiment using a glass jar rather than the ziplock bags.

ROLL IT! SHAPE IT!

4 INSTRUCTIONS

1 Put the cream and the salt in one qt.-size ziplock bag. Remove as much air as possible and seal the bag well. Put this bag inside the second qt.-size bag, again removing as much air as possible and sealing it well. (Double-bagging will help to prevent leakage.) Shake the bag vigorously, checking the seal now and then.

2 After 3 to 4 minutes, the cream will start to thicken. Continue shaking. When your arm gets tired, get your friend to take over! After about 15 minutes, butter will start to form, and the mixture will look like a scrambled egg with milky water.

3 Open the bag slightly at one corner and pour off the liquid (great for baking and drinking). Squeeze the butter in the bag to remove any more liquid. When you've drained away as much liquid as you can, scrape the butter from the bag (it will be quite soft) and onto the baking parchment paper. You can pat it dry with a paper towel if necessary.

4 Use the parchment to shape the butter into a roll. Wrap it in the parchment. Store in the fridge.

THE SCIENCE SCOOP

Imagine that you could shrink to the size of a water molecule and go swimming in a cup of milk. Everywhere you turned, the milk would be full of what looked like water balloons. On closer inspection, you'd see that the balloons were filled with fat and that the rubbery outside layers were membranes sealing the fat inside. Over time, these fat globules float up to the surface of the milk. The top layer of milk, with all that fat, is called cream.

To make butter, you have to tear open the membranes that surround the fat so the fat can ooze out and clump together. So you shake or churn the cream. You're left with one big clump of fat, which is butter, and some thin liquid. Take a sip of the liquid. If you did a thorough job of ripping those membranes open, you'll have fat-free skim milk.

FAT GLOBULES

FAT LEAKS OUT AND FORMS BIGGER CLUMPS

RICOTTA CHEESE

> Difficulty level
> **Grab a grown-up!**

> Active time needed
> **30 minutes**
> Additional time: 60-90 minutes

SEPARATING PROTEIN MOLECULES

Making cheese is another way to unmix milk. In Block o' Butter (p. 12), you pulled out the fat to create butter. When you make ricotta cheese, it's the proteins doing the clumping. You can think of proteins as sheets of origami paper. Normally, the proteins are folded up tight. But if you heat them and add vinegar, they unfold. Try this ricotta recipe and watch a different milk transformation take place.

SUPPLIES
Large fine-mesh strainer, large bowl, fine-woven muslin or cheesecloth, large saucepan, measuring cups and spoons, candy thermometer, wooden spoon, slotted spoon, sealable plastic container

INGREDIENTS
8 cups whole milk
½ cup heavy cream
1 tsp. salt
¼ cup distilled white vinegar
  or lemon juice

TIP
For an accurate reading, be sure to use a candy thermometer.

2

3

WATCH FOR IT!
The milk will form a soft, clumpy cheese, which is ricotta!

INSTRUCTIONS

1 Set the strainer over the bowl and line it with the muslin or cheesecloth. Set it aside.

2 Combine the milk, cream, and salt in the saucepan. Set the pan over medium heat, stirring often to prevent the mixture from sticking to the bottom of the pan and burning, until the temperature of the mixture reaches between 175°F and 180°F on the candy thermometer.

3 Remove the pan from the heat and slowly add the vinegar or lemon juice, stirring gently. As soon as all the vinegar or lemon juice has been added, stop stirring and let the mixture sit undisturbed for about 20 minutes. The milk solids will coagulate, clump, or float to the surface, leaving the liquid underneath.

4 Spoon the solids into the strainer, leaving behind as much liquid as you can in the saucepan.

5 Let the mixture sit, without pressing on the curds, until most of the liquid has drained away—about an hour. If it's still dripping, leave it for another 15–20 minutes until it stops.

6 Spoon the ricotta from the cloth into the plastic container. The ricotta will keep for about 1 week in the refrigerator.

THE SCIENCE SCOOP

Hidden inside the folds of milk proteins are connection points, which are kind of like bits of Velcro. Heat and vinegar cause the proteins to unfold. Suddenly, the connection points are exposed. As the proteins bump into each other, they hook together, forming a solid. Fats, sugars, and other parts of the milk get trapped in the tangle of proteins. Presto, you've got milk you can bite into.

TIP
Try your ricotta with pizza or lasagna, or add it to some fruit and honey.

WATER PURIFIER

Difficulty level
Medium

Active time needed
10 minutes
Additional time: 4–6 hours

SEPARATING WATER MOLECULES FROM A MIXTURE

You can go for weeks without food but for only a few days without water. So getting clean drinking water is one of the most important unmixing jobs on Earth. Water from lakes, streams, or the ocean is a mixture that may contain bacteria, salt, dirt, or harmful chemicals. Water treatment plants clean the water for drinking. In this activity, you will contaminate water with salt and food coloring. Then you'll build your own water treatment plant and separate clean, drinkable water from the mix.

SUPPLIES
Clear glass bowl, sunny location, drinking cup, plastic wrap, small stone, drinking straw

INGREDIENTS
Water
Salt
Food coloring

1

THE SCIENCE SCOOP

As the sun warms the bowl of water, water molecules near the surface get hot enough to evaporate. Some of the evaporated water floats to the top of the bowl and lands on the plastic wrap. Those molecules condense on the plastic wrap and drip down into the cup. Salt and food coloring molecules would need to be much hotter than water to evaporate, so they stay in the bowl. When you stick your straw in the cup, you've got clean, clear water.

INSTRUCTIONS

1 Fill a clear glass bowl about half full of water. Mix in a spoonful of salt and 3 or 4 drops of food coloring.

2 Set the bowl of water outside in a very sunny place where it will not be disturbed. This works best on a hot day.

3 Place a drinking cup that's shorter than the bowl in the center of the bowl of water. Cover the bowl, with the cup inside, with plastic wrap.

4 Set the stone on top of the plastic wrap just above the cup. The plastic wrap should slant downward from the sides of the bowl toward the cup.

5 Leave your water purification system in the sun for 4–6 hours. Then, carefully remove the plastic wrap and stone. Stick a drinking straw into the cup and take a drink.

TIP
Make sure no contaminated water gets into the cup as you set up and take apart your system.

1

3

> EVAPORATE: to change from a liquid into a gas

LET'S WATCH HOW TO SEPARATE MIXTURES

BONUS: METAL FOR BREAKFAST

When you take a deep breath, you draw oxygen into your lungs. From there, the oxygen moves into blood vessels and is absorbed by red blood cells. Inside the red blood cells, the oxygen connects to the iron atoms in an important molecule called hemoglobin. The hemoglobin holds the oxygen tight, like a seat belt, as the red blood cells whisk it around your body. Iron is so important that manufacturers sometimes take unusual approaches to including it in food. In this experiment, you'll find out if your cereal maker is adding metal to your breakfast.

WATCH FOR IT!
Tiny iron filings will stick to your magnet.

YOU NEED

TIME
5 minutes

SUPPLIES
Mortar and pestle, strong magnet (such as a rare-earth magnet), small plastic bag, cup of water

INGREDIENTS
Breakfast cereal that has 100% of the recommended daily allowance (RDA) of iron (look at the nutrition panel on the packaging)

INSTRUCTIONS

1 Put a handful of cereal into the mortar. Use the pestle to crush the cereal into a fine powder. The finer the powder, the better your results.

2 Put the magnet in the plastic bag and pull the bag tight around it. Slowly drag the magnet through the crushed cereal. Some of the cereal dust will stick to the magnet.

3 Keeping the plastic bag wrapped around the magnet, dip it into the cup of water. Swish it around to rinse the cereal particles away. Don't worry, the iron will not wash off.

4 Look closely at your plastic bag for a cluster of black dust.

THE SCIENCE SCOOP

Iron is naturally found in meat and some vegetables. In those foods, the iron exists as one part of a large molecule, such as hemoglobin. However, the easiest way for a food manufacturer to increase the iron content of a product is to add pure, metallic iron. Many cereal makers grind iron into metal dust and mix it into the batter for their flakes. When you pass a magnet through ground cereal that contains iron dust, the iron is attracted to the magnet. You can see the metal filings and move them around with your magnet.

CHAPTER TWO

SOLIDS, LIQUIDS, AND YUM!

>>

Eat a frozen juice pop on a hot summer day, and you can see it changing from a solid to a liquid. The molecules of your juice are the same, whether they are frozen on a stick or dripping onto the sidewalk. They just behave differently. In solid form, the molecules hold on to each other tightly, and the pop keeps its shape. As the molecules heat up, they begin to move. They loosen their grip and slip past one another, becoming a liquid. Liquid molecules take the shape of the container they are in. In this chapter, you'll see how the behavior of solids and liquids can be surprisingly delicious.

BAKED ALASKA

INSULATION FROM HEAT

> Difficulty level
> **Grab a grown-up!**

> Active time needed
> **25 minutes**

NOTE
Use whatever flavor of cake and ice cream you prefer.

Everybody knows that ice cream melts if you don't eat it fast. As soon as you take ice cream out of the freezer and into room temperature, the water molecules in the ice cream warm up and start moving. Soon they are moving too fast to stay together as a solid. But what if you knew a trick that could keep the ice cream firm even in a hot oven? In this recipe, you'll experiment with insulation, or material that makes it difficult for heat to move from one place to another.

YOU NEED

SUPPLIES
Knife, baking sheet, ice cream scoop, large bowl, electric mixer, measuring cups and spoons, large spoon

INGREDIENTS
4 thick slices from a store-bought jelly roll or 4 store-bought sponge cake rounds, about 3 inches in diameter
4 scoops ice cream
2 egg whites, at room temperature
Pinch of cream of tartar
½ cup sugar

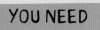

THE EGG WHITES EXPAND—WITH AIR!

Make sure you use pasteurized (or safe) eggs for this recipe.

INSTRUCTIONS

1 If you're using a jelly roll, get an adult to help you slice it in four pieces. Place the jelly roll or sponge cake slices well apart on the baking sheet. Put a generous scoop of ice cream on top of each slice. Transfer the baking sheet to the freezer.

2 Set an oven rack in the middle of the oven and preheat it to 425°F. To make a meringue, put the egg whites into a clean bowl and, using an electric mixer, whisk them until soft peaks form when you lift the beaters.

3 Sprinkle the cream of tartar into the egg whites. Then add half the sugar and whisk until the mixture is glossy. Add the remaining sugar 1 Tbsp. at a time, whisking well between additions, until all the sugar has been added and the mixture is stiff and glossy.

THE SCIENCE SCOOP

The process of whisking mixes air into egg whites to make meringue. As the meringue stiffens, the air is trapped in small bubbles. Heat does not move easily through trapped air. It stays on whichever side it started on. So the warmth of the oven doesn't get to the ice cream. Materials that keep heat from traveling are called insulators. The cake beneath the ice cream also has trapped air within it. Since the ice cream has insulation above and below, it stays cold.

continued >>>

BAKED ALASKA

INSULATION FROM HEAT

>>>continued

INSTRUCTIONS

4 To assemble the baked Alaska, remove the baking sheet from the freezer and quickly spoon the meringue over the ice cream, making sure to cover the ice cream and the edges of the cake completely with a thick layer. You can make it pretty by adding peaks in the meringue: Touch it with the back of the spoon, then lift.

5 Get an adult's help to transfer the baking sheet immediately to the middle of the hot oven and cook until the meringue is set and golden, 3–4 minutes. Ask an adult to help to remove it from the oven. Carefully transfer the Baked Alaska from the baking sheet to a serving dish, and eat it right away.

TIP
Make sure there are no gaps between the meringue and the cake.

4

WATCH FOR IT!
The meringue comes out of the oven browned and warm, but the ice cream doesn't melt!

5

LET'S WATCH HOW TO INSULATE LIQUIDS

BONUS: KEEP IT WARM

Suppose you wanted to bring soup to school for your lunch. What would be the best way to keep it warm until it was time to eat? In Baked Alaska (p. 20), we saw how meringue works as an insulator. In this experiment, we'll test two possible insulators, using warm water to represent your soup.

WATCH FOR IT!
The water wrapped in a wool sock will be warmer!

YOU NEED

TIME
30 minutes

SUPPLIES
2 identical containers with lids, cooking thermometer, 1 wool sock, aluminum foil

INGREDIENTS
Very warm water

INSTRUCTIONS

1 Fill the identical containers with equal amounts of very warm water. Measure the temperature in both containers to make sure they start out the same.

2 Fasten the lids tightly and slide one container into the wool sock. Wrap the other container tightly with the foil, keeping the foil as smooth as possible.

3 Leave both containers in the same place for 15 minutes. Then remove them from their coverings and measure their temperatures to see which covering did a better job of keeping the water warm. Then make a lovely glass of peppermint tea!

THE SCIENCE SCOOP

Heat is a form of energy. That energy makes the molecules in your hot water wiggle and jostle each other. If you just left the hot water on the counter, the water molecules would bump against molecules in the air and on the countertop. With each bump, the water molecules would pass some of their energy to surrounding molecules, slowing—and cooling—them. Insulators work as barriers that prevent the energy from being passed on. Metal, such as aluminum foil, is a poor insulator because energy moves easily between metallic molecules. Wool, on the other hand, contains fibers and pockets of air that slow the movement of energy. To find the perfect way to insulate your water, try repeating this experiment with other materials you have around the house, like a scarf or a washcloth.

MAPLE CANDY

Difficulty level
Grab a grown-up!

Active time needed
30 minutes
Additional time: 1 hour

FORMATION OF SOLID CRYSTALS

You're familiar with water turning into ice. Water freezes at 32°F, a temperature that is not very comfortable for people. The freezing point for sugars, on the other hand, is very high. Even at room temperature, sugars are solid, like ice. This is why you don't have to worry about sugar melting in your kitchen cabinet.

Maple syrup contains both water and sugar. In this experiment, you'll heat up maple syrup to evaporate some of the water. With the water out of the way, the sugar molecules can get together. You can watch them freeze into a solid, with no freezer required.

TIP
For an accurate reading, be sure to use a candy thermometer.

YOU NEED

SUPPLIES
Heavy baking sheet, large and heavy-bottomed saucepan, silicone spatula, candy thermometer, wooden spoon, magnifying glass

INGREDIENTS
Vegetable oil, for greasing the baking pan
2 cups pure maple syrup

WATCH FOR IT!
The syrup will harden as it cools.

3

CRYSTALS FORMING

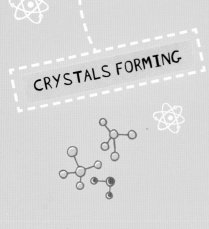

INSTRUCTIONS

1 Lightly grease the baking sheet with vegetable oil and set it aside. Have an adult help you with the next steps. In the saucepan, bring the maple syrup to a boil over medium-high heat, stirring occasionally with the silicone spatula. Boil until the syrup reaches 250°F on the candy thermometer. Be careful, and don't leave it unattended, as the syrup will foam up in the pan. To reduce foaming, stir carefully with the spatula.

2 Remove the pan from the heat and let it cool to 170°F without stirring, about 10 minutes.

3 Using the wooden spoon, stir the mixture, which will be stiff, then pour or scrape it onto the greased pan. Let it set for up to 1 hour.

continued >>>

MAPLE CANDY
CRYSTALLINE SOLID FORMATION

>>>continued

THE SCIENCE SCOOP

Grab a magnifying glass and take a close look at your maple candy. You'll see that it is shaped into smooth-sided blocks. These blocks are called crystals. Crystals form when molecules stack themselves into repeating patterns. The particular shape made by the sugar crystals in maple syrup is a cube. The size of the crystals depends on how quickly the syrup cools. Syrup that cools slowly forms large crystals, because the molecules have lots of time to line up in groups before they reach their freezing point. When syrup cools quickly, the molecules freeze in smaller clusters.

CHECK THE STRUCTURE

○ CARBON
◐ OXYGEN
○ HYDROGEN

CRYSTALS FORM FROM PATTERNS OF REPEATING MOLECULES, SUCH AS THIS SUCROSE MOLECULE.

> CRYSTAL: a solid in which the molecules are arranged in a repeating pattern

LET'S WATCH CRYSTAL FORMATION

BONUS: SMALL ANIMAL SALT LICK

WATCH FOR IT!
As the paper dries, crystals will form wherever you painted the salt solution.

You can grow large salt crystals in much the same way as sugar crystals. You can even paint them into a design. Remember, this is edible only for animals—you should NOT eat it. A pet gerbil or hamster will find this irresistible and nutritious.

YOU NEED

TIME
10 minutes, plus drying overnight

SUPPLIES
Measuring cups and spoons, heatproof mug, thick black poster board, paintbrush

INGREDIENTS
½ cup hot water
3–4 Tbsp. table salt

INSTRUCTIONS

1 Put the hot water in the mug and gradually add the salt very slowly, stirring until dissolved.

2 Dip the paintbrush in the salty liquid and paint a picture on the black poster board.

3 Leave it to dry overnight, by which time a salty picture will emerge. Put it out for your pet hamster or gerbil to eat!

THE SCIENCE SCOOP

As the water dries up, only the salt molecules are left on the poster board. They organize themselves into orderly crystals as they dry. On paper, the salt crystals form thin layers of small crystals. Scientists have also experimented with growing thin layers of salt crystals—in space! Without gravity pulling them down, the molecules do a better job of organizing themselves into perfect shapes. So for perfect crystals, you'll have to take a trip to the space station.

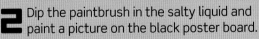

BEEF JERKY

OSMOSIS—WATER MOVING OUT OF FOOD

> Difficulty level
> **Grab a grown-up!**

> Active time needed
> **10 minutes**
> Additional time: 6 hours or overnight

A steak is the muscle of a cow, so it is made of muscle cells. You can think of muscle cells as having two parts: the solid fibers that feel chewy in your mouth and the liquid juices. The liquid portion is mostly water. Other molecules, including flavor, salt, vitamins, and minerals, are dissolved in the water.

When meat rots, it is because bacteria have begun to grow on the muscle fibers. However, most bacteria need water to survive. So if you remove the water from the steak, you'll have beef jerky that can last a long time before it goes bad.

YOU NEED

SUPPLIES
Sharp knife, measuring cups and spoons, large ziplock bag, baking pan, tongs

INGREDIENTS
1½ lb. thick flank steak
1¼ cups soy sauce
¾ cup water
2 tsp. freshly ground pepper
3 garlic cloves, crushed
2 Tbsp. honey

TIP
For easier slicing, you can freeze the steak for 1½ hours before cutting it.

THE SCIENCE SCOOP

The liquid portion of a muscle cell has lots of water molecules and not very many other molecules. Scientists call this having a high concentration of water. Soy sauce, on the other hand, has lots of flavor and salt molecules dissolved in it. Soy sauce, therefore, has a lower concentration of water. All of these molecules are constantly moving around, but water molecules have an advantage. They are small enough to move through the membrane, or lining, that surrounds the muscle cells. Water molecules tend to move from areas of high concentration to areas of low concentration. So, in this recipe, water molecules leave the muscle cell and move into the soy sauce. From there, the hot oven causes the water to evaporate.

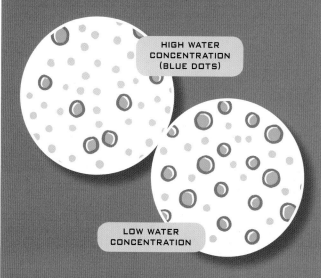

HIGH WATER CONCENTRATION (BLUE DOTS)

LOW WATER CONCENTRATION

INSTRUCTIONS

1 With an adult, use a sharp knife to slice the flank steak against the grain into thin strips.

2 Mix together the remaining ingredients in the ziplock bag and add the sliced meat. Seal the bag and squeeze and shake it to coat the steak. Refrigerate it for at least 4 hours, or preferably overnight.

3 After 4 hours, remove the upper oven rack and place a baking pan on the lower oven rack to catch drips. Preheat the oven to 200°F.

4 Remove the steak slices from the marinade, allowing excess juices to drip off, and lay them directly on the top oven rack in a single layer. The meat will have firmed up. Return the upper rack with the beef on it to the oven. Cook the beef slowly for 2 hours (or up to 4 hours, for extra-crispy jerky).

WATCH FOR IT! When the meat comes out of the oven, it will be stiff and dry.

OSMOSIS: movement of water from an area of high concentration to one of low concentration

FRUIT-AND-NUT COUS-COUS

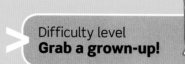

> Difficulty level
> **Grab a grown-up!**

> Active time needed
> **10 minutes**

OSMOSIS—WATER MOVING INTO FOOD

WATCH FOR IT!
The couscous and fruit will swell and soften as they absorb the water.

You saw in Beef Jerky (p. 28) that water moves from where there is a high concentration of water molecules to where there is a low concentration. Scientists call that movement of water osmosis. In this recipe, the higher concentration is in the pot of water, while the food has almost no water in it.

YOU NEED

SUPPLIES
Measuring cups and spoons, large bowl, saucepan, large plate, small frying pan, wooden spoon, fork

INGREDIENTS
1 cup couscous
2 Tbsp. raisins
2 Tbsp. dried apricots, chopped
Salt and freshly ground pepper
1¼ cups chicken broth or vegetable broth or water
2 Tbsp. sliced almonds
2 Tbsp. butter

INSTRUCTIONS

1 Put the couscous, raisins, and apricots in the bowl. Sprinkle with 2 tsp. salt.

2 Have an adult help you boil the broth or water in the saucepan and pour it into the bowl. Stir to combine.

3 Cover the bowl with the plate and let it stand for 5 minutes.

4 Meanwhile, have an adult help you put the almonds in the frying pan over medium heat. Cook, stirring often, until golden, about 2 minutes. Add the butter and stir so it melts.

5 Using a fork, stir the nuts and butter into the couscous mixture. Season to taste with salt and pepper and let it cool.

WATER CONCENTRATION: the ratio of water molecules to other molecules in a solution

THE SCIENCE SCOOP

Water in this experiment moves from the area of high concentration to the area of low concentration. In this case, the higher concentration was in the pot of water, while the food had almost no water in it.

Heating the water speeds up the process of osmosis. Heat is a form of energy. When molecules get warm, they have more energy for movement, and they move faster. With boiling temperatures, it only takes a few minutes to replace the water that the manufacturers removed from the couscous and dried fruit.

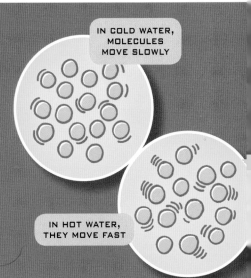

IN COLD WATER, MOLECULES MOVE SLOWLY

IN HOT WATER, THEY MOVE FAST

LET'S WATCH HOW JUICE IS MADE

BONUS: JUICY FRUIT SALAD

We've seen osmosis at work in Beef Jerky (p. 28) and Fruit-and-Nut Couscous (p. 30). Osmosis can also help make syrup for fruit salad. We'll use sugar to lessen the concentration of water outside the fruit and to draw water out of the fruit into our syrup.

YOU NEED

TIME
30 minutes

SUPPLIES
Measuring cups and spoons, knife, medium bowl, large spoon or rubber spatula, dish towel

INGREDIENTS
½ cup strawberries
½ cup raspberries
2 small peaches
½ cup blueberries
1 Tbsp. sugar
A good squeeze of lemon juice

TIP
If berries aren't available, try with other fruits.

WATCH FOR IT!
The fruit will lose some juice into the bowl, creating a sweet, liquidy syrup.

INSTRUCTIONS

1 Have an adult help you to cut the strawberries in half and to pit and chop the peaches.

2 Put all the fruit in the bowl. Sprinkle it with the sugar and the lemon juice.

3 Toss the fruit together gently, cover the bowl with the dish towel, and set it aside for 20 minutes. Serve the fruit salad with some yogurt.

THE SCIENCE SCOOP

Fruit cells are like little bags full of water and other molecules. In this recipe, a little juice spills out of the cells as you chop. When you add sugar, you lower the concentration of water in that juice. Water moves out of the fruit into the fruit juice until the ratio of water molecules to sugar molecules has evened out, and you have a juicy, syrupy salad.

CHAPTER THREE

IT'S A GAS!

>> Pucker your lips and blow out a stream of air. That air is made up of gas molecules, which spread out to fill whatever space is available to them. You have to capture gases if you don't want them to escape. Most gases are invisible yet very powerful. In this chapter, we'll look at what happens when we trap and release gases in different foods.

DANCING SOUP

DISSOLVED GASES

> Difficulty level
Easy

> Active time needed
5 minutes

TIP
Make sure the pieces are no bigger than a raisin!

When you drink a soda, the fizzy feeling in your mouth comes from bubbles of a gas called carbon dioxide. Carbon dioxide becomes acidic when it is dissolved in water, and soda is mostly water. When the acid hits your mouth, it triggers a nerve response at receptors that sense heat and pain. Scientists aren't sure why the burning sensation of fizz is enjoyable. Whatever the reason, you can enjoy watching and drinking carbon dioxide in this fizzy soup.

1

YOU NEED

SUPPLIES
Kitchen scissors, bowl

INGREDIENTS
Dried apricots
Dried cranberries
Raisins
Lemon-lime soda

THE SCIENCE SCOOP

Dried fruit is denser than soda, so pieces of fruit sink to the bottom of a bowl of soda. When bubbles of carbon dioxide bump into the rough surface of the dried fruit, they get trapped. Tiny bubbles merge and become larger bubbles. Eventually, enough gas gathers below a piece of dried fruit to lift it to the surface. At the top, some of the gas escapes, and the fruit sinks. The cycle continues until most of the carbon dioxide has escaped and the soda is flat.

> DENSITY: how heavy something is for its size

INSTRUCTIONS

1 Cut the dried apricots with kitchen scissors into raisin-size pieces.

2 Combine the apricots, cranberries, and raisins in a bowl.

3 Pour the lemon-lime soda over the fruit.

WATCH FOR IT!
The fruit pieces will wiggle, float to the top, and then sink. In a moment, they'll repeat their performance.

WATCH THEM DANCE!

POPOVER POPS

GAS UNDER PRESSURE

> Difficulty level
Grab a grown-up!

> Active time needed
15 minutes
Additional time: 40 minutes

When a gas heats up, its molecules move faster. They bounce off each other and spread farther apart. Bakers have been putting expanding gas to work for hundreds of years to make fluffy bread. When you make popovers, you use expanding hot air to blow up a roll as if it's a batter balloon.

YOU NEED

SUPPLIES
Measuring cups and spoons, large bowl, whisk, 12-cup muffin pan

INGREDIENTS
1 cup flour
2 tsp. salt
Freshly ground pepper
4 eggs
1¼ cups milk
½ cup vegetable oil

TIP
Pour gently so that you don't splash hot oil out of the pan.

1

3

> EVAPORATE: when liquids are heated so much that they become gases

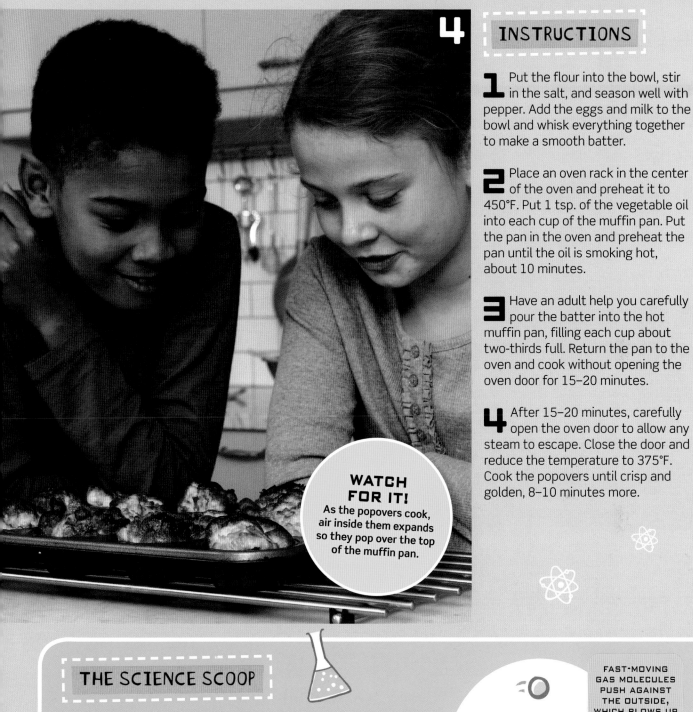

WATCH FOR IT!
As the popovers cook, air inside them expands so they pop over the top of the muffin pan.

INSTRUCTIONS

1 Put the flour into the bowl, stir in the salt, and season well with pepper. Add the eggs and milk to the bowl and whisk everything together to make a smooth batter.

2 Place an oven rack in the center of the oven and preheat it to 450°F. Put 1 tsp. of the vegetable oil into each cup of the muffin pan. Put the pan in the oven and preheat the pan until the oil is smoking hot, about 10 minutes.

3 Have an adult help you carefully pour the batter into the hot muffin pan, filling each cup about two-thirds full. Return the pan to the oven and cook without opening the oven door for 15–20 minutes.

4 After 15–20 minutes, carefully open the oven door to allow any steam to escape. Close the door and reduce the temperature to 375°F. Cook the popovers until crisp and golden, 8–10 minutes more.

THE SCIENCE SCOOP

When popover batter is poured into a preheated pan, the outside starts cooking right away. Proteins and starches from the flour and eggs form a tight seal as they cook. Meanwhile, the heat causes the liquid from the eggs and milk to evaporate, or turn into a gas. The gas presses against the outside layer of batter but cannot get through. Instead, the outside layer stretches and inflates like a balloon. The resulting popover has a crisp outside and a light, fluffy inside.

FAST-MOVING GAS MOLECULES PUSH AGAINST THE OUTSIDE, WHICH BLOWS UP LIKE A BALLOON.

POPCORN BLAST

GAS PRESSURE EXPLOSION

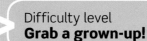
> Difficulty level
> **Grab a grown-up!**

> Active time needed
> **10-15 minutes**

A kernel of corn is the seed of a corn plant. It contains the embryo of a plant, along with moisture and starch, which will provide energy for the new plant as it sprouts. When you cook popcorn, the outside of the seed, called the seed coat, quickly toughens and forms a seal. Because the moisture and starch are trapped inside, it sets the stage for a small explosion.

YOU NEED

SUPPLIES
Measuring spoons and cups, large and deep saucepan with a (preferably clear) lid, large serving bowl

INGREDIENTS
3 Tbsp. vegetable oil
⅓ cup popcorn kernels
2 Tbsp. butter, or to taste, melted
Salt

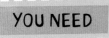

THE SCIENCE SCOOP

When you heat popcorn, the moisture inside the kernel evaporates and becomes a vapor, or gas. As the popcorn becomes hotter, the molecules of water vapor move faster and farther apart. Since gas molecules are not connected to one another the way molecules in liquids and solids are, they spread out rapidly and press against the seed coat. Eventually, the pressure is so great that the kernel explodes.

STEAM BUILDS UP.

THE STEAM PRESSURE FORCES THE KERNEL TO EXPLODE!

WATCH FOR IT!
As each kernel gets hot enough, it will pop and fluff out.

THE SEED TURNS INSIDE OUT!

INSTRUCTIONS

1 Get an adult to help you put the oil in the saucepan over medium heat. Heat the oil gently for 2–3 minutes.

2 Add the popcorn kernels carefully. Get an adult to help you shake the pan gently so they are all in a single layer. Cover the pan and remove it from the heat for 30 seconds.

3 Put the covered pan back over medium heat. The popping should begin soon after, and once it does, gently shake the pan, moving it from side to side. If you can, keep the lid slightly ajar to allow steam to escape. Once the popping slows so there are several seconds between pops, immediately pour the popcorn into the serving bowl. Drizzle with the butter, sprinkle with salt to taste, and enjoy.

After you watch these small explosions, you get to eat them!

> **PRESSURE: the force of one thing pushing on another**

EGG IN A BOTTLE
ATMOSPHERIC PRESSURE

SAFETY NOTE
The bottle may be hot
from the fire. Let it cool for
a moment before touching it.

There's a lot of air on your head right now. All the air from where you are standing up to the outer atmosphere 100 miles above Earth is pressing down on your head. It weighs as much as a polar bear. But you don't feel like you have a polar bear on your head because your body pushes back with equal pressure. It's hard to believe that all this air could really be so strong, because you can't see it or feel it. In this activity, you can use that air pressure to create an unusual egg snack.

YOU NEED

SUPPLIES
2 birthday candles, bottle with an opening slightly smaller than an egg, matches, iced tea spoon

INGREDIENTS
1 hard-boiled egg

WATCH FOR IT!
After a moment, the egg will slide into the bottle all by itself.

INSTRUCTIONS

1 Peel the hard-boiled egg. Rinse away any bits of shell.

2 Stick the birthday candles into the fatter end of the egg.

3 Have an adult light the candles for you.

4 Get your bottle and hold it upside down over the burning candles for about 30 seconds so that the air is warmed.

5 Quickly stick the end of the egg with the candles into the top of the bottle, making a tight seal. Flip the bottle over and set it down. The candles will go out by themselves. Wait until the egg slides into the bottle.

6 Serve the egg, inside the bottle. Your friend will need an iced tea spoon to eat it! Remind him or her not to eat the candles!

TIP
Some iced coffee drinks come in bottles with an opening that is slightly smaller than a large egg.

THE SCIENCE SCOOP

If you just set an egg on top of a bottle, air pressure won't push it in. There is air inside the bottle pressing back against the air above the bottle. But when you burn candles inside the bottle, the air in the bottle gets hot and expands. Some of the air moves out of the bottle. When you cover the top of the bottle with the egg, it seals the opening. As the air inside the bottle cools, it contracts and takes up less space in the bottle. Suddenly the air pressure outside the bottle is higher than the pressure inside the bottle. The outside pressure pushes on the egg, and the egg slides into the bottle.

INFLATABLE MARSHMALLOW

> **Difficulty level**
> **Medium**

> **Active time needed**
> **5 minutes**

REDUCING AIR PRESSURE

Marshmallows feel spongy in your mouth because they are full of tiny pockets of air. The air pressure in a marshmallow is usually balanced against the air pressure in the atmosphere. In this experiment, you can see what happens to a marshmallow when you upset that balance.

YOU NEED

SUPPLIES
Cotton swab, small glass jar, modeling clay, straw, mirror

INGREDIENTS
Food coloring
1 marshmallow

1 Dip the cotton swab into the food coloring and use it to draw a face on one side of the marshmallow.

2 Place the marshmallow inside the jar.

3 Wrap a clump of modeling clay around the straw.

4 Insert the straw into the jar and add extra clay as needed to seal the top of the jar completely around the straw. Blow gently into the straw to make sure it is completely sealed.

5 Place the mirror in such a way that you can see your marshmallow inside the jar while the straw is in your mouth. Now, use the straw to suck as much air as you can out of the jar. Watch your marshmallow in the mirror.

6 Release the straw from your mouth. Watch how the marshmallow responds.

TIP
Not all experiments work on the first try, and this one is tricky. If it doesn't work at first, perhaps try thicker clay and a narrower-necked bottle.

WATCH FOR IT!
When you suck on the straw, the marshmallow will swell, stretching out the face you drew. When you release the straw, the marshmallow will deflate.

THE SCIENCE SCOOP

As you suck through the straw, you remove air from the jar. Then the air surrounding the marshmallow has lower pressure than the air inside the marshmallow. Because gases spread out to fill whatever space is available, the gases inside the marshmallow's air pockets spread out, pushing the sides of the marshmallow out with them. When you release the straw, air rushes back into the jar and squashes the marshmallow back down.

5

ONE BAD APPLE
HORMONES AND RIPENING

> Difficulty level
> **Easy**

> Active time needed
> **5 minutes**
> Additional time: 12 hours

When a pear first forms, growing on a tree, it starts out as a hard and sour fruit. Over time, it grows and ripens. For most fruits, the ripening process continues even after the fruit is picked. But ripening fruit has a neat trick—it can cause other fruit to ripen as well, hence the saying "One bad apple ruins the bunch." In this experiment, we'll use a ripe banana to make unripe pears become soft and sweet.

YOU NEED

SUPPLIES
Paper bag

INGREDIENTS
2 unripe pears
1 very ripe banana

INSTRUCTIONS

1 Place one of the unripe pears on a table or countertop where air can circulate freely.

2 Place the other pear and the banana into the paper bag, and roll the top of the bag so that it stays closed. Leave all three fruits overnight.

3 In the morning, compare the pear from the paper bag with the pear that sat on the counter overnight.

WATCH FOR IT!
The pear in the bag with the banana will be softer and riper than the pear on the counter.

THE SCIENCE SCOOP

Inside a plant, there are chemicals called hormones that tell the parts of the plant when to grow and develop. You have hormones inside your body controlling growth and development, as well. But the hormones in your body are dissolved in your blood. The plant hormone that controls ripening is a gas. When one fruit releases the ripening gas, it affects all the fruit around it. When you trap the gas that comes from a ripe banana in a bag with an unripe piece of fruit, the banana's hormones will cause the unripe fruit in the bag to ripen more quickly than unripe fruit outside the bag.

CHAPTER FOUR

ACTIONS
AND
REACTIONS

>> Sometimes when you mix ingredients, their molecules rearrange. Atoms break off from molecules, or molecules that were separate might join together. When molecules rearrange, we call it a chemical reaction. In this chapter, you'll set chemical reactions into motion.

COLOR-CHANGING COOKIES

MEASURE THE pH BALANCE

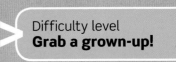
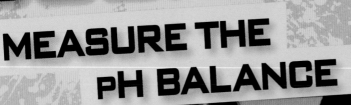

Don't worry—these cookies aren't cabbage-flavored, they're just cabbage-colored. The color in purple cabbage comes from a color molecule called a pigment. Pigment molecules reflect certain colors of light. In this case, the cabbage pigment reflects red and blue light to appear purple. You'll start by cooking up a batch of cabbage juice. Then you can make the cookies, and reveal cabbage's secret power.

1

2

YOU NEED

SUPPLIES
Knife, measuring cups and spoons, saucepan, slotted spoon, sieve or colander, cup, mixing bowls, wooden spoon or electric mixer, cup, baking sheet, spatula

PART 1 INGREDIENTS
½ head purple cabbage
About 3 cups water

PART 2 INGREDIENTS
½ cup butter, softened
⅓ cup sugar
1½ cups flour
1 tsp. baking powder
10 Tbsp. milk
1 tsp. lemon juice

3

PART ONE

Concoct cabbage juice

1 Have an adult help you thinly slice your cabbage. Add it to the saucepan with the water.

2 Place the saucepan over high heat and bring the water to a boil. Boil the cabbage for 5 minutes, then remove it with a slotted spoon and keep boiling until the liquid has reduced to about ½ cup and the color is very dark.

3 Remove the saucepan from the heat and let it cool. Using the sieve or colander, strain the water into a cup. While the juice cools, make the cookies.

TIP
The longer you boil the cabbage juice, the darker it will be. Dark juice is key for colorful cookies. It should appear almost black when you look at it through a clear glass.

MIX TO CHANGE THE pH BALANCE

4

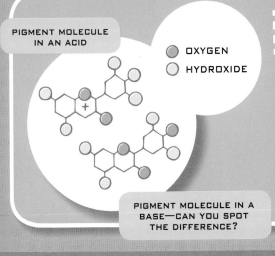

PIGMENT MOLECULE
IN AN ACID

○ OXYGEN
○ HYDROXIDE

PIGMENT MOLECULE IN A
BASE—CAN YOU SPOT
THE DIFFERENCE?

THE SCIENCE SCOOP

The pigment in purple cabbage reflects purple light because of its shape. When the pigment is mixed with an acid—lemon juice—a chemical reaction occurs that changes the shape of the pigment molecule. The new shape reflects pink light. You may think of acids as dangerous chemicals that can burn your skin, and very strong acids certainly can be dangerous. But a lot of foods are acidic, including lemon juice and just about anything else that tastes sour. Even vanilla is mildly acidic, which is why it isn't included in this recipe.

continued >>>

COLOR-CHANGING COOKIES

MEASURE THE PH BALANCE

>>>continued

PART TWO

Put on your baker's hat

1 Preheat the oven to 350°F. Cream the butter with the sugar in a mixing bowl, using either the wooden spoon or the electric mixer.

2 Sift the flour and baking powder into the bowl and mix them in. The mixture should resemble coarse bread crumbs.

3 Divide the mixture between two bowls. In one bowl, add 3 tsp. of the cooled cabbage juice and 5 Tbsp. of the milk. Stir.

4 In a cup, mix together 2 tsp. of the cabbage juice and the lemon juice. The color change is startling! Add that mixture to the second bowl. Add the remaining 5 Tbsp. of milk and stir it in.

5 Drop tablespoonfuls of the two mixtures onto a baking sheet. Bake until set and golden at the edges, 10–12 minutes. Get an adult to help you remove the cookies from the oven and transfer them to a wire rack to let cool.

COLOR CHANGES!

WATCH FOR IT!
One set of cookies should be purple, and the other set should be pink!

LET'S WATCH A REACTION HAPPEN!

BONUS: COLOR TRICKS

> **BASE: a substance with a pH greater than 7**

Purple cabbage juice has another trick up its sleeve. If you mix it with food that is basic, it turns blue. If you mix it with a very strong base, it will even turn green. Let's try mixing your left-over cabbage juice with various foods to see what colors you can make.

YOU NEED

TIME
10 minutes

SUPPLIES
Clear glass jars, glasses, or test tubes

INGREDIENTS
Leftover purple cabbage juice (from Color-Changing Cookies, p. 46)
Egg whites or baking soda (bases)
Other food and drink you have on hand

INSTRUCTIONS

1 Pour your leftover cabbage juice into several clear jars, glasses, or test tubes.

2 Select a food to add to each jar or test tube. Start with some egg white or baking soda.

3 Stir the juice and food together, and observe.

WATCH FOR IT!

If your cabbage juice turned red or pink, the food was an acid. If it turned blue or green, you're face-to-face with a base.

PH SCALE

ACID ← → BASE

THE SCIENCE SCOOP

Scientists use the pH scale to describe how strong an acid is. A substance with a pH below 7 is an acid, and the lower the number, the stronger the acid. A substance with a pH above 7 is called a base. A pH of 7 describes something, like pure water, that is neutral: neither an acid nor a base.

Acids taste sour, while bases taste bitter. More of our foods are sour acids than bitter bases. In fact, one reason humans (especially kids) tend to dislike bitter flavors is that many poisons happen to be bitter.

BANANA BREAD

MIX AN ACID WITH A BASE

You can harness the power of acids and bases for all kinds of kitchen tricks: Both acidic and basic molecules are highly reactive, which means they easily change into new substances. In this recipe, buttermilk is an acid and baking soda is a base. Let's mix them together and find out how a chemical reaction helps to create banana bread.

YOU NEED

SUPPLIES
9x5-inch loaf pan, baking parchment paper, measuring cups and spoons, mixing bowls, whisk, sieve, skewer, spatula

INGREDIENTS
½ cup vegetable oil, plus more for greasing the pan
2 eggs
⅓ cup buttermilk
1 cup mashed bananas (about 3 small ones)
2 tsp. finely grated orange zest
1½ cups sugar
1¾ cups flour
1 tsp. baking soda
½ tsp. salt
½ cup chopped walnuts

> CHEMICAL REACTION: when the atoms in chemicals rearrange to make something new

CARBON DIOXIDE INSIDE

1

THE SCIENCE SCOOP

A molecule of baking soda consists of one sodium atom, one hydrogen atom, one carbon dioxide molecule, and an extra oxygen atom. When it is exposed to an acid, like buttermilk, a chemical reaction breaks down the baking soda and releases carbon dioxide gas. These tiny bubbles of gas press out against the batter and puff it up, leaving the baked bread soft and fluffy. The other parts of the baking soda molecule remain in the bread, including the sodium, so too much baking soda will make your bread taste salty.

continued>>>

BANANA BREAD

MIX AN ACID WITH A BASE

>>>continued

> BATTER: the mixed-up ingredients that will turn into cake or bread after they have been baked

INSTRUCTIONS

1 Preheat the oven to 325°F. Generously grease the loaf pan and line its base with baking parchment paper.

2 In a large bowl, whisk together the eggs, buttermilk, oil, bananas, and orange zest.

3 In another bowl, sift together the sugar, flour, baking soda, and salt. Add the dry ingredients to the banana mixture along with the walnuts.

4 Mix well and pour the batter into the prepared pan. It will come only about halfway up the sides of the pan.

5 Bake for 1 hour 20 minutes, then get an adult's help to test whether a skewer inserted in the center of the bread comes out clean. Bake for up to 10 minutes more, if needed. Have the adult remove the banana bread from the oven, and let it cool in the pan.

MEASURE HEIGHT

WATCH FOR IT!
When the bread comes out of the oven, notice how tall it is. The loaf rises during baking.

LET'S WATCH A REACTION HAPPEN!

BONUS: ORANGE SODA

When you make banana bread, the chemical reaction between baking soda and acid takes place in the batter. This experiment will give you a chance to see it in action while you make yourself a healthy fizzy drink.

YOU NEED

TIME
5 minutes

SUPPLIES
Drinking glass, spoon

INGREDIENTS
1 pinch baking soda
1 cup orange juice

INSTRUCTIONS

1 Drop a pinch of baking soda into a drinking glass.

2 Pour in the orange juice. Stir to combine.

3 Drink up, because once a fizzy drink is open to the air, the carbon dioxide escapes and the drink loses its fizz.

WATCH FOR IT!
Tiny bubbles will form in the drink and rise to the surface. Take a swig! The drink will feel fizzy in your mouth.

THE SCIENCE SCOOP

Orange juice is an acid. When it hits the baking soda, it kicks off the same chemical reaction that took place in the banana bread batter. With no flour or bananas in the way, you can see the bubbles of carbon dioxide as they form. Colas and other soft drinks are also fizzy because they are filled with bubbles of carbon dioxide.

HONEYCOMB TOFFEE

EXPERIMENT WITH AN ACID

> Difficulty level
> **Grab a grown-up!**

> Active time needed
> **20 minutes**

WATCH FOR IT!
When you add the baking soda, the sugar solution will fizz and bubble. You need a big pot to make sure it doesn't bubble over! When the candy cools, there will be holes where the bubbles were.

When you made Banana Bread (p. 50), you saw that carbon dioxide caused the batter to puff up. In this old-fashioned candy recipe, you'll see a similar reaction, but here, vinegar causes the baking soda to break down. Like buttermilk, vinegar is an acid. In fact, vinegar's scientific name is acetic acid. That name may not sound yummy, but honeycomb toffee sure is!

YOU NEED

SUPPLIES
8-inch square baking pan, measuring cups and spoons, large stockpot or Dutch oven, wooden spoon, candy thermometer, oven mitts

INGREDIENTS
Vegetable oil, for greasing the pan
2 cups sugar
4 Tbsp. white vinegar
3 Tbsp. light corn syrup
2 cups water
1 tsp. baking soda

> **SOLUTION:** a mixture where one substance is dissolved in another

Add baking soda and watch it fizz!

1 Grease the pan with oil and set it aside.

2 Pour the sugar, vinegar, corn syrup, and water into the stockpot or Dutch oven. With an adult's help, place the pot over medium-high heat and stir constantly with a wooden spoon as you bring the mixture to a boil.

3 Use the candy thermometer to watch the temperature of the solution. When it reaches 285°F, remove the pot from the heat.

4 Add the baking soda to the pot and stir.

5 Immediately pour the mixture into the prepared pan. Let it sit until it cools completely.

SAFETY NOTE

The melted sugar will be extremely hot as you pour it from the pot into the pan. Use oven mitts to protect your hands and make sure you do not drip any melted sugar on your skin.

TIP

Leave the syrup as it falls in the pan. Do not spread it, or you will pop the bubbles that are forming.

THE SCIENCE SCOOP

In your candy mixture, vinegar (the acid) causes baking soda (the base) to break down and form carbon dioxide. Both acids and bases break into new molecules with ease. Sugar, on the other hand, is a much more stable molecule, so sugar stays out of the chemical reaction. The sugar does melt, however, and this forms a liquid to trap the carbon dioxide bubbles. The gas bubbles create pockets inside the candy that remain as the sugar cools and hardens around them, giving the candy a satisfying crunch.

JIGGLING GELATIN

REARRANGING MOLECULES

> Difficulty level
Grab a grown-up!

> Active time needed
10 minutes
Additional time: 1–2 hours

WATCH FOR IT!
As the gelatin cools, the liquid will change into a gel.

Inside a mouthful of gelatin is a tangle of molecules. While it feels smooth when you are eating it, gelatin actually started out as animal bones! In bones, the super-long molecules twist together in orderly sets of three. Other chemicals, including calcium, stiffen the twists to make the bones sturdy and strong. Store-bought gelatin powder has been removed from bones and dried. In this recipe you'll make gelatin molecules react to each other and turn liquid into gel.

DISSOLVE THE GELATIN

YOU NEED

SUPPLIES
Measuring cups and spoons, large glass baking dish, kettle, wooden spoon

INGREDIENTS
2 Tbsp. unflavored gelatin powder
1 .16-oz. packet unsweetened powdered drink mix, any flavor
¾ cup sugar or sweetener, or to taste

INSTRUCTIONS

1 Put 1 cup of cold water into the glass baking dish. Sprinkle in the gelatin powder and let it soften for 5 minutes.

2 Meanwhile, bring a kettle of water to a boil and have an adult help you measure out 2 cups of boiling water.

3 Add the powdered drink mix to the baking dish with the gelatin. Add in about ¾ cup sugar.

4 Add the 2 cups hot water to the baking dish and stir well until everything is dissolved. Add another 1 cup of cold water, so there's 4 cups of liquid in total.

5 Taste the mixture and add more sugar if needed. Refrigerate until set, 1–2 hours.

THE SCIENCE SCOOP

Picture a box of spaghetti. In the box, the noodles lie straight, in rows. But after the spaghetti noodles are cooked and stirred, they sit in a tangled clump on your plate. This is similar to what happens to gelatin molecules when they are heated with hot water. The heat unwinds the neat gelatin twists, leaving loose gelatin molecules swirling in the water. As the gelatin cools, the molecules try to rearrange themselves into neat twists, but they don't all line up properly. Instead, they wind up in a tangled web. The water is trapped inside the web of gelatin molecules, so it can't slosh around, and this combination of solid and liquid gives your snack a smooth feel.

GELATIN MOLECULES BEFORE HEATING

AFTER HEATING

CLUMPING CRANBERRIES
CREATING A GEL

Difficulty level
Grab a grown-up!

Active time needed
15-20 minutes

You sit down to Thanksgiving dinner with a plate of turkey and cranberry sauce. Delicious! In some families, the traditional cranberry sauce is thick but runny. Other families prefer their cranberry sauce as a firm gel. The ingredients for both sauces are the same! The difference is how much of a special chemical reaction you allow to take place. Find out the secret to both sauces in this experiment.

TIP
Stir frequently so the sauce on the bottom doesn't burn.

2

YOU NEED

SUPPLIES
Measuring cups, saucepan, wooden spoon, jar, bowl for serving

INGREDIENTS
½ cup lightly packed brown sugar
½ cup orange juice
2 cups cranberries, fresh or frozen

THE SCIENCE SCOOP

You learned in Jiggling Gelatin (p. 56) about the long gelatin molecules from bones that become tangled to form a gel. Cranberries contain a different molecule, called pectin, which works in much the same way. In nature, pectin helps hold plant cells together. In the kitchen, pectin can strengthen your cranberry sauce. When you heat cranberries in water, some of the pectin comes out of the berries. The longer you heat the cranberries, the more pectin enters the water, and the firmer your sauce.

There is a catch. The easiest chemical reaction for the pectin molecule is to combine with water, rather than with other pectin molecules. So you have to add some sugar, which occupies the water molecules. Then the pectin molecules will attach to each other and thicken the sauce. At the same time, the sugar gives those mouth-puckeringly tart cranberries a taste to be thankful for.

WATCH FOR IT!
The first batch yields a soft, goopy sauce. The second forms a firm gel.

INSTRUCTIONS

1 Combine the sugar and orange juice in a saucepan and bring it to a boil over medium-high heat.

2 Add the cranberries and continue to simmer until most are tender but still holding their shape, about 5 minutes if using fresh cranberries and 8–10 if using frozen.

3 Remove half of the mixture to a bowl. Set it aside to cool.

4 Continue to simmer the remaining sauce over medium heat, mashing the berries down and stirring often, for 4–5 more minutes. By this time the cranberries will have broken down further and the sauce will be thicker.

5 Pour the thicker sauce into the jar and set it aside in the refrigerator until cold. The sauce in the jar should be served cold, but the softer sauce can be warmed through before serving in a bowl.

LET'S WATCH: FROM WATER TO SLIME

BONUS: FIBER SLIME

The seed of the psyllium plant has a quirk. A fiber molecule in the seed reacts with water, expanding as it joins with more and more water molecules. The molecule can swell to many times its original size. This ensures that the seed has enough water to grow. You can watch a small amount of psyllium fiber react with a cup of water to make fabulous slime.

YOU NEED

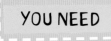

TIME
15 minutes

SUPPLIES
Microwavable bowl, oven mitts

INGREDIENTS
1 Tbsp. psyllium-based fiber supplement
1 cup water
Food coloring (optional)

INSTRUCTIONS

1 Combine the fiber supplement, water, and a few drops of food coloring, if using, in a large microwavable bowl.

2 Microwave the mixture on high for 5 minutes. Watch it as it cooks. If it bubbles over the side, stop the microwave and let it cool briefly before continuing.

3 Use the oven mitts to remove the bowl from the microwave. The slime will be very hot. Let it sit for at least 5 minutes before touching it.

WATCH FOR IT!
The liquid will transform into a smooth slime.

TIP
Try experimenting with the amount of water you add to the psyllium powder. Less water will make the slime rubbery, and more water will make it gooier.

THE SCIENCE SCOOP

If you could zoom in on psyllium fiber, pectin (p. 58), or gelatin (p. 56) molecules, you would see that they all look a little bit like chains of paper clips. All three molecules contain short segments that repeat over and over again. Long molecules with repeating parts are called polymers. People usually use polymers of psyllium fiber to draw extra water into their intestines—it turns out that this slippery slime can also help a bowel movement slide out with ease. But don't eat this slime, it will make you feel sick!

CHAPTER FIVE

BIOLOGY IN YOUR KITCHEN

>>

In your kitchen, right now, you probably have several items that were made by nonhuman living things. Yogurt, sauerkraut, and some cheeses are formed by bacteria. Fungi grow in your kitchen too—to help make bread! But how do you really know what you are tasting? Let's explore how biology shapes your food.

MYSTERY MERINGUE

SEEING AND TASTING

WATCH FOR IT!
Most people will say the orange-colored meringue has an orange flavor and the yellow-colored meringue has a lemon flavor.

You may know that your nose plays an important part in tasting. In this experiment, you'll see that your eyes do too. Ask your friends to take a taste test of these two treats. They'll be surprised when what they taste doesn't match what they see.

YOU NEED

SUPPLIES
2 baking sheets, baking parchment paper, 2 mixing bowls, electric mixer, measuring cups and spoons, grater, rubber spatula, large spoon

INGREDIENTS
4 egg whites, at room temperature
1 cup superfine sugar
Pinch of cream of tartar
1 tsp. finely grated orange peel
1 tsp. finely grated lemon peel
¼ tsp. orange food coloring
¼ tsp. yellow food coloring

TIP
Make sure your friend doesn't see you making the meringues, or else another part of the brain will kick in and say, "I'm being tricked!"

3 Continue adding the remaining sugar about 1 Tbsp. at a time until all the sugar has been added and the mixture is thick and glossy.

4 Divide the mixture into the two bowls. Add the orange peel and yellow food coloring to one bowl, and the lemon peel and orange food coloring to the second. Gently fold each mixture with a rubber spatula just until the peel is mixed through (don't worry if the color is marbled).

5 Drop large spoonfuls of the meringue onto each prepared baking sheet (use one sheet for orange flavor and one sheet for lemon flavor). Get an adult's help to transfer the baking sheets to the oven. Cook for 30 minutes, then reduce the oven temperature to 250°F and cook for another 30 minutes. Reduce the heat to 200°F and cook for 30 minutes more. Turn the oven off and leave the meringues in the oven until they are cold.

6 Have an adult help to remove the baking sheets from the oven. The meringues should peel easily from the parchment. Give your friends the taste test.

INSTRUCTIONS

1 Preheat the oven to 275°F. Line the baking sheets with the parchment paper and set them aside.

2 In a large, clean bowl, whisk the egg whites using an electric mixer until stiff peaks form when you lift the beaters. Add ½ cup of the sugar and the cream of tartar and beat until they are incorporated.

THE SCIENCE SCOOP

When a flavor molecule attaches to one of your taste buds, the taste bud sends a message along a nerve to the brain. When an odor molecule attaches to a sensory cell in the nose, the nose sends that information along a different nerve to the brain. Your eyes send even more information, and your brain sorts through all the signals to decide what you are tasting. Scientists once thought that the brain used only taste and smell to identify food, but recent research shows that when the brain gets conflicting information, the eyes sometimes win.

SIGHT + TASTE + SMELL = FLAVOR

MOCK APPLE PIE

FOOLING YOUR SENSES

> Difficulty level
Grab a grown-up!

> Active time needed
30 minutes
Additional time: 45 minutes

Manufacturers rely on flavors and colors to create enjoyable foods. Sometimes the real flavor or color is too expensive or doesn't react well with the other ingredients. In that case, the manufacturer will figure out which chemicals in the food create the characteristic flavor and find other sources for those chemicals. In this recipe, you can create the taste, appearance, and aroma of apple pie ... with no apples!

YOU NEED

SUPPLIES
9-inch pie dish or tart pan, large saucepan, measuring spoons and cups, knife

INGREDIENTS
2 ready-made refrigerated or frozen
  pie dough rounds, softened
  according to package directions
2 cups water
1½ cups sugar
1½ tsp. cream of tartar
25 round buttery crackers, such
  as Ritz
½ tsp. cinnamon
2 Tbsp. butter, cut into small chunks

1

THE SCIENCE SCOOP

Lots of information comes together in your brain to cause you to taste apple pie in this recipe. Your eyes signal your brain that it looks like an apple pie. Your nose detects the smell of cinnamon, which you associate with apple pie. When you bite in, the crackers provide a texture that is similar to that of apple pie. Cream of tartar adds the final touch. Cream of tartar contains tartaric acid. Apples contain a variety of acids, often including tartaric acid. Acids connect with taste buds to send a "sour" signal to your brain. The combination of this information leads your brain to conclude that you are eating apple pie. Are you surprised that your brain can be fooled so easily?

TASTES LIKE APPLES!

WATCH FOR IT!
The pie will look, smell, and taste like an apple pie.

INSTRUCTIONS

1 Use one of the pie dough rounds to line the pie dish or tart pan. Set it aside in the refrigerator until needed.

2 Preheat the oven to 425°F. Get an adult's help to bring the water to a boil in the saucepan over high heat. Mix together the sugar and cream of tartar. Get help to add this to the boiling water, and stir until it's dissolved. Next, add the crackers. Do not stir. (The crackers will stand in for apples in the finished pie.) Boil for 3 minutes, then remove the pan from the heat.

3 Get an adult to help you carefully pour this mixture into the prepared pie dish or tart pan. Sprinkle the cinnamon over top and dot it with the butter. Use the remaining pie dough round to top the pie, crimping the edges with your fingers or the tines of a fork to seal. Feel free to decorate the pie, but be sure to put in a steam hole.

4 Bake until the pastry is golden brown, 25–30 minutes. Get an adult to remove the pie from the oven, and let it stand for 15 minutes before eating.

TRICK YOUR SENSES

> Difficulty level
Easy

> Active time needed
10 minutes

ALTERING CELL PROPERTIES

WATCH FOR IT!
At first you will mainly taste the sugar, but when the candy has been in your mouth for a while, determining the flavor may become easier.

When you pop a piece of hard candy into your mouth, your saliva goes to work dissolving the various candy molecules, which will bump into your taste buds. You can see the bumps that hold the taste buds on your tongue, but you also have them on the roof of your mouth, your throat, and even at the top of your esophagus. These taste buds contain specialized cells for tasting. However, those cells don't react with as many flavors as you might think. In this experiment, you'll see the limits of your sense of taste.

YOU NEED

SUPPLIES
Brown paper bag

INGREDIENTS
Hard candy in a variety of flavors

INSTRUCTIONS

1 Unwrap the candies and put them into the brown paper bag.

2 Close your eyes and hold your nose with one hand.

3 With your other hand, reach into the bag and pull out a piece of candy. Don't peek! Place the candy on your tongue and let it dissolve. See if you can tell what flavor it is.

4 Still holding your nose, let the candy dissolve in your mouth for 1 minute. See if time helps you figure out what flavor it is.

5 Look at the candy. Were you right?

THE SCIENCE SCOOP

When a sugar connects with a taste cell, it sends a message to the brain that says "sweet!" Your taste cells are a bit like puzzle pieces. They connect only with molecules that match in shape, and they have only a few slots for connections. Taste cells can join with molecules that are sweet, sour, salty, bitter, or a savory flavor known as umami. The rest of what you think of as flavor actually comes from your nose. Your smelling cells have slots that fit many kinds of molecules. After the candy has been on your tongue for a bit, some of the molecules drift into your nose through the back of your throat. When your sense of smell kicks in, you can identify the candy's "flavor."

LET'S WATCH HOW ODORS ARE MADE

BONUS: ARTIFICIAL STRAWBERRIES

Have you ever wondered how you can have a candy that tastes and smells like strawberries but doesn't have any strawberries in it? Food companies make artificial flavors and artificial scents based on the chemicals found in real food. You can make your own artificial strawberry scent using chemicals found in common foods.

YOU NEED

TIME
About 5 minutes

SUPPLIES
Measuring cups and spoons, knife, food processor

INGREDIENTS
¼ cup fresh snap peas
½ Gala or Golden Delicious apple, cut into chunks
2 Tbsp. brown sugar

> **ARTIFICIAL: an imitation of something natural**

WATCH FOR IT!
Sniff really carefully, and you will notice the strawberry smell!

INSTRUCTIONS

1 Have an adult help you put the snap peas, apple, and brown sugar into a food processor and blend until they are well chopped together. Remove the lid and sniff!

THE SCIENCE SCOOP

A strawberry contains lots of different kinds of chemical molecules. The sensing cells in your mouth and nose have slots for only a few of them, so your brain thinks "strawberry flavor" based on just the handful of chemicals that fit those slots. Food companies have figured out that they don't need whole strawberries to make strawberry flavor. They need only a collection of those chemicals that we can taste and smell. The ingredients in this recipe include many of the same distinctive molecules that produce a strawberry smell. Taste it, however, and you will see how different your taste and smell receptors can be!

GROW YOUR OWN YOGURT

COOK WITH BACTERIA

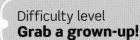

> Difficulty level
> **Grab a grown-up!**

> Active time needed
> **30 minutes**
> Additional time: 8 hours

You'll notice that there aren't many ingredients in this recipe. That's because bacteria do most of the work in yogurt making. Natural yogurt tastes sour because the bacteria have already eaten the sugar! In the process, they produce lactic acid. Lactic acid is a waste product of bacteria, but it is great for yogurt makers, because it changes the texture of milk into that smooth yogurt consistency. As the scientist/cook, your job is to set up the conditions for the bacteria to grow.

YOU NEED

SUPPLIES

Measuring cups and spoons, saucepan, candy thermometer, large bowl, small bowl, wide-mouthed thermos with a capacity of at least 2 cups, jars or plastic pots with lids

INGREDIENTS

2 cups milk (any kind will do, though whole milk will make thicker yogurt)
Ice
3 Tbsp. store-bought plain yogurt (make sure it says "live cultures" on the label)

1

TIP
Enjoy with fresh fruit and honey!

INSTRUCTIONS

1 Put the milk into the saucepan and clip the thermometer inside the pan. With the help of an adult, place the pan over medium-high heat and, stirring often, heat until the milk reaches 185°F.

2 While the milk is heating, fill the large bowl with cold water and ice. When the milk reaches 185°F, set the pan in the bowl. Let the milk cool to 110°F. In a small bowl, mix 3 Tbsp. of the milk with the store-bought yogurt until smooth, then add this mixture to the cooled milk. Mix well.

3 Meanwhile, fill the thermos with hot tap water. Let it stand for 5 minutes so that the thermos is warmed through. Discard the water and transfer the cooled milk mixture to the thermos. Seal and let it stand at room temperature for about 8 hours (you can leave it longer, though the flavor will become sharper and stronger tasting).

4 Transfer the finished yogurt to clean jars or plastic pots and store in the refrigerator for up to 1 week.

WATCH FOR IT!
As the yogurt stands, it will become thick.

THE SCIENCE SCOOP

The first step in yogurt making is to heat the milk. The heat kills any harmful bacteria that may be in the milk already. Recall from Ricotta Cheese (p. 14) that milk contains clusters of protein bundles. Heating the milk causes those bundles to fall apart. Next, you cool the milk to a temperature that works well for bacteria growth. You add a bit of yogurt from an existing batch to introduce some living yogurt bacteria to your milk. Those bacteria go to work, eating the milk sugars and producing lactic acid. The lactic acid causes the proteins to join together in a big web, which gives the milk a firmer texture. When the yogurt is firm enough, you cool it down. When bacteria get cold, they stop eating and producing lactic acid, and your yogurt is done.

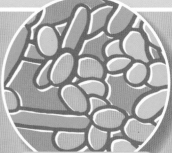

SQUIGGLY YOGURT BACTERIA

BREAD ON THE RISE

FUNGI IN THE KITCHEN

> Difficulty level
> **Grab a grown-up!**

> Active time needed
> **30 minutes**
> Additional time: 2–2½ hours

TIP
If the dough starts to stick to you as you knead, rub more flour on your hands.

People have been making bread for thousands of years, but it wasn't until after the invention of microscopes that scientists were able to discover the organisms called yeast that make bread rise. Yeast are fungi, so they are related to mushrooms. But they are much smaller: Each yeast organism has only one cell. In the old days, people would save a pinch of uncooked dough to get yeast to make their next loaf. Today, you can buy packaged yeast at the store. In this recipe, you'll see how yeast can make a lump of dough rise, swell, and double in size.

THE SCIENCE SCOOP

Yeast eat sugar. They use the natural sugars in flour for energy, and in the process, they make carbon dioxide gas. As soon as the yeast have moisture and flour available, they start eating. Carbon dioxide gas bubbles out of the yeast cells and becomes trapped in pockets of thick and sticky dough. The dough stretches to make room for the carbon dioxide, and the loaf rises. Look closely when you cut your bread, and you'll see that the fluffy texture comes from the hundreds of tiny holes in each slice.

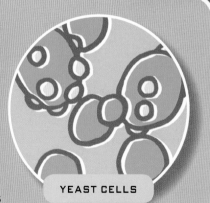

YEAST CELLS

YOU NEED

SUPPLIES

2-lb. loaf pan, measuring cups and spoons, 2 large bowls, wooden spoon, stand mixer (optional), dish towel or plastic wrap, plastic shopping bag

INGREDIENTS

Olive oil, for greasing the pan
3 cups whole-wheat bread flour, plus extra for dusting
2 tsp. salt
1 tsp. brown sugar
2 tsp. rapid-rise yeast
About 1½ cups warm water

INSTRUCTIONS

1 Generously grease the loaf pan with olive oil and set it aside.

2 Put the flour into one of the bowls. Add the salt, sugar, and yeast and mix well to distribute them evenly through the flour.

3 Make a well in the middle of the flour mixture and add about 1¼ cups of the warm water. Mix into a dough, starting off with a wooden spoon and then using well-floured hands to bring the dough together, adding the remaining water if necessary.

4 Tip the dough out onto a lightly floured surface and knead until it is smooth, elastic, and no longer sticky, 5–10 minutes. Alternatively, use a stand mixer fitted with a dough hook to knead it for 6–8 minutes.

5 Form the dough into a ball and put it into a clean, oiled bowl, turning it to coat with oil. Cover the bowl with a clean dish towel or plastic wrap and let it rise in a warm place until it has doubled in bulk, 1–1½ hours.

WATCH IT RISE!

continued >>

BREAD ON THE RISE

FUNGI IN THE KITCHEN

>>> continued

WATCH FOR IT!
The dough rises until the bread puffs over the top of the pan.

6 Turn the dough out of the bowl onto a clean surface and knead it briefly. Shape the dough into an oblong shape about the same length as your pan. Transfer the dough to the pan, pressing into the corners.

7 Sprinkle the top of your loaf with a little flour, then put the dough inside a plastic shopping bag until it rises to the top of the pan, 30–60 minutes. Meanwhile, preheat the oven to 450°F.

8 Remove the pan from the bag. Transfer the dough to the oven and bake it for 40–45 minutes. When it is a rich golden brown, get an adult to take the bread out of the oven.

9 Get an adult to remove the bread from the pan and check that the bread sounds hollow when it's tapped on the bottom. If not, return it to the oven for another 10 minutes. Once it is cooked, allow it to cool completely in the pan before slicing and serving.

IT GREW!

LET'S WATCH YEAST EAT AND GROW

BONUS: PET YEAST

If you have ever had a pet or raised a plant, you know that all living things need certain essentials to survive. A pet needs food and shelter. A plant needs water and sun. Well, yeast are also alive. If you look at a packet of yeast, you'll see small tan balls. Each ball is a collection of living yeast cells. If you feed the yeast cells and make them a comfortable home, you can raise a colony of yeast that will make great pets—at least for an afternoon.

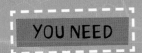

YOU NEED

TIME
35 minutes

SUPPLIES
Measuring cup, thermometer, teaspoon

INGREDIENTS
⅔ cup warm water (100°F–115°F)
1 tsp. active dry yeast
1 tsp. sugar

INSTRUCTIONS

1 Use a thermometer to make sure that your water is the correct temperature. If the water is too hot, the yeast will die. If it is too cold, they won't grow.

2 Add the yeast and sugar to the warm water. Stir.

3 Allow the mixture to sit for at least 30 minutes. Check it regularly to see how it changes.

WATCH FOR IT!
In about half an hour, the top of the mixture will be covered in foam.

THE SCIENCE SCOOP

When you purchase dry yeast, the yeast cells are alive but not doing much. They don't have the food, water, or temperature that they need, so they are resting. Scientists call it being dormant, and it's similar to the way that some animals hibernate. The yeast cells come out of their resting state when they are put in warm water and given sugar to eat. When yeast cells use sugar for energy, they create carbon dioxide gas as waste. You can see that your yeast are active by watching for bubbles (of carbon dioxide) to collect at the top of the cup. Don't eat this; it doesn't taste good!

SAUERKRAUT

BACTERIA MAKING FOOD

Some bacteria cause food to spoil, but other bacteria are helpful in food production. In the days before refrigeration, people found lots of ways to protect their food from unhealthy bacteria. One way was to encourage healthy bacteria to take over the food and prevent unhealthy bacteria from moving in. In this experiment, you'll set up an environment that is just right for the healthy bacteria that normally live on cabbage leaves to flourish. In exchange, those bacteria will make a delicious pot of sauerkraut.

1

YOU NEED

SUPPLIES
Sharp knife or food processor, large bowl, measuring cups and spoons, food-grade sauerkraut pot or ceramic pot, linen cloth, plate that just fits inside your pot, can of beans to act as a weight

INGREDIENTS
1 purple cabbage
1 green cabbage
3 Tbsp. table salt
3 tart apples, such as Granny Smiths, cored and sliced
10 cracked juniper berries (optional)

THE SCIENCE SCOOP

Fortunately, one big difference separates healthy bacteria from unhealthy bacteria—healthy bacteria can survive without oxygen. Covering the cabbage with liquid removes most of the available oxygen, so unhealthy bacteria cannot survive. The healthy bacteria eat the sugars in the cabbage and produce the flavor molecules that give sauerkraut its distinctive taste. You can safely eat the sauerkraut at any time, but traditional recipes allow about 3 weeks to give the bacteria time to digest most of the sugar.

SAFETY NOTE
If your sauerkraut is slimy, do not eat it!
Unhealthy bacteria produce slime.

WATCH FOR IT!
Over time, the cabbage will take on the classic sour flavor of sauerkraut.

1 Ask an adult to help you to use a sharp knife or food processor to shred the cabbage. Put it in the bowl and mix in the salt. (The salt draws water from the cabbage and creates the brine in which it ferments and sours without rotting.) Stir in the sliced apples and cracked juniper berries, if using.

2 Put the mixture into the clean sauerkraut pot or ceramic pot, leaving at least 2 inches at the top. Wet the linen cloth and use it to cover the pot. Place the plate on top of the cloth. Put the can of beans on top of the plate. This will force the brine to rise high enough to reach the cloth. If this hasn't happened after 24 hours, make a brine by dissolving 1 Tbsp. of salt in 1½ cups water and add enough of this to cover the cabbage (some cabbage, particularly in winter, contains less water).

3 Leave the sauerkraut to ferment. It is best to leave your sauerkraut in a cool place such as a cellar. Every day, take off the can of beans, remove the plate, and skim off any scum from the surface. Replace the damp cloth every few days. If the room and water are kept at 60°F, the fermenting process will take at least 1 month. To check if it is ready, wait at least 2 weeks. Then, taste the sauerkraut. Once it has developed a sourness that is pleasing to you, it is ready.

4 When you are happy with the flavor, place the sauerkraut mixture in a large pan and bring to a boil over medium heat. Remove it from the heat and ladle the hot sauerkraut into jars. Let it cool, then label the jars before storing for up to 12 months.

MEALWORM BROWNIES

> Difficulty level
Grab a grown-up!

> Active time needed
35–45 minutes
Additional time: 24 hours

INSECTS AS PROTEIN

From a scientific perspective, insects make excellent food. They are low in fat and high in protein, fiber, and other nutrients. Raising insects also puts less strain on the environment than raising other animals that we use for meat. A cow, for example, has to be fed about eight pounds of food for every pound of meat that the farmer can get from it. Insects need only about two pounds of food to produce a pound of meat. Insects also need less water and produce fewer harmful waste products. Food scientists are hopeful that insects may solve some of our future food needs, but you can get a head start with this recipe.

YOU NEED

SUPPLIES
Small plastic container with a lid, colander, baking sheet, mixing bowl, wooden spoon, baking pan

INGREDIENTS
About 25 yellow mealworms (available at pet stores and bait shops)
Rolled oats, if needed (see step 1)
Ready-made brownie mix

THE SCIENCE SCOOP

A mealworm is the larva, or young version, of a darkling beetle. Just as a caterpillar becomes a butterfly, a mealworm will become a pupa and then emerge as an adult beetle. Beetles, especially their larvae, are the most commonly eaten insects in the world. As you bite into your brownie, rest assured that you are in good company. More than 2 billion people from countries around the world include insects in their diets.

THIS IS WHAT YOUR MEALWORMS GROW INTO.

1 Open the package of mealworms and remove any that are dead. If the mealworms are packed in bran, oats, or cornmeal, proceed to step 2. Fill a small plastic container with rolled oats and poke a few air holes in the lid. Move the mealworms into the plastic container and close the lid. Leave the mealworms at room temperature for 24 hours. During this time, they will eat the rolled oats, which will replace the paper in their intestines.

2 Put the mealworms in the freezer for 20 minutes. Preheat the oven to 200°F.

3 Remove the mealworms, rinse them in the colander, and then spread them on the baking sheet. Bake the mealworms for 1 hour. Let them cool, then break each mealworm into 2 or 3 pieces.

4 Prepare the brownie mix according to the package directions. Before you bake the brownies, stir in your toasted mealworm pieces.

5 Bake the brownies as instructed. Enjoy!

WATCH FOR IT!
The mealworms add a nutty flavor and crunch to the brownies.

GREAT PROTEIN SOURCE!

GLOSSARY

Acid: a substance with a pH less than 7

Artificial: an imitation of something natural

Atom: a tiny particle that makes up all matter

Bacteria: a family of microscopic, single-celled organisms that lack a nucleus

Base: a substance with a pH greater than 7

Batter: the mixed-up ingredients that will turn into cake or bread after they have been baked

Carbon dioxide: a common gas that is made of one carbon atom and two oxygen atoms

Chemical: a substance made of a defined group of atoms

Chemical reaction: when the atoms in chemicals rearrange to make something new

Concentration: the amount of one chemical compared with the amount of the others in a mixture

Condense: to turn from a gas into a liquid

Crystal: a solid in which the molecules are lined up in a repeating pattern

Density: how heavy something is for its size

Emulsifier: a molecule that connects to both water and oil

Evaporate: to change from a liquid into a gas

Fungi: a group of living things, including mushrooms and yeast, that digest plant and animal matter for food

Insulation: material that slows the flow of heat

Larva: a young insect that differs in form and sources of nutrition from the adult of its species

Membrane: a thin covering

Molecule: a group of connected atoms

Osmosis: movement of water from an area of high concentration to one of low concentration

pH: a measure of how acidic or basic a chemical is

Pigment: a molecule that absorbs some colors of light and reflects others, giving a substance the appearance of color

Polymer: a large molecule formed by connecting many identical, small molecules

Pressure: the force of one thing pushing on another

Solution: a mixture in which one substance is dissolved in another

Water concentration: the ratio of water molecules to other molecules in a solution

FURTHER READING

Also by National Geographic

National Geographic Kids Cookbook: A Year-Round Fun Food Adventure, by Barton Seaver

Try This: 50 Fun Experiments for the Mad Scientist in You, by Karen Romano Young

And on the Web

exploratorium.edu/cooking

sciencebuddies.org

kids.nationalgeographic.com/explore

kids.nationalgeographic.com/explore/try-this

kids.nationalgeographic.com/explore/cookbook

SCIENCE STANDARDS

Each chapter of this book has been correlated with the Next Generation Science Standards (NGSS), which were developed by the National Research Council and are based on the Framework for K–12 Science Education. These standards describe important scientific ideas and practices that all students should learn and incorporate with relevant science, technology, engineering, and math (STEM) concepts.

The outline below lists each chapter's main ideas and matches those ideas with related NGSS life (L), physical (P), or Earth and space science (ESS) standards for grades 3 through 8. After each standard description, you'll notice a series of numbers and letters. These represent the grade level, subject area, and standard number. For example: 4-ESS1-1 translates into grade four, Earth and space science, standard number one. For more details on NGSS, visit nextgenscience.org.

CHAPTER 1: MIXING AND UNMIXING
Pages 5–18
Main Ideas: combining and separating mixtures
Standards:
- Develop a model to describe that matter is made of particles too small to be seen. (5-PS1-1)
- Make observations and measurements to identify materials based on their properties. (5-PS1-3)
- Develop models to describe the atomic composition of simple molecules and extended structures. (MS-PS1-1)

CHAPTER 2: SOLIDS, LIQUIDS, AND YUM!
Pages 19–32
Main Ideas: heat and states of matter
Standards:
- Develop a model to describe that matter is made of particles too small to be seen. (5-PS1-1)
- Measure and graph quantities to provide evidence that regardless of the type of change that occurs when heating, cooling, or mixing substances, the total weight of matter is conserved. (5-PS1-2)
- Develop a model that predicts and describes changes in particle motion, temperature, and state of a pure substance when thermal energy is added or removed. (MS-PS1-4)

CHAPTER 3: IT'S A GAS!
Pages 33–44
Main Ideas: heating gases, air pressure
Standards:
- Measure and graph quantities to provide evidence that regardless of the type of change that occurs when heating, cooling, or mixing substances, the total weight of matter is conserved. (5-PS1-2)
- Plan and conduct an investigation to provide evidence of the effects of balanced and unbalanced forces on the motion of an object. (3-PS2-1)
- Develop a model that predicts and describes changes in particle motion, temperature, and state of a pure substance when thermal energy is added or removed. (MS-PS1-4)
- Plan an investigation to provide evidence that the change in an object's motion depends on the sum of the forces on the object and the mass of the object. (MSPS2- 2)

CHAPTER 4: ACTIONS AND REACTIONS
Pages 45–60
Main Ideas: chemical reactions
Standards:
- Conduct an investigation to determine whether the mixing of two or more substances results in new substances. (5-PS1-4)
- Analyze and interpret data on the properties of substances before and after the substances interact to determine if a chemical reaction has occurred. (MS-PS1-2)

CHAPTER 5: BIOLOGY IN YOUR KITCHEN
Pages 61–77
Main Ideas: interpreting sensory information, movement of matter
Standards:
- Use a model to describe that animals receive different types of information through their senses, process the information in their brain, and respond to the information in different ways. (4-LS1-2)
- Develop a model to describe the movement of matter among plants, animals, decomposers, and the environment. (5-LS2-1)
- Gather and synthesize information that sensory receptors respond to stimuli by sending messages to the brain for immediate behavior or storage as memories. (MS-LS1-8)
- Develop a model to describe the cycling of matter and flow of energy among living and nonliving parts of an ecosystem. (MS-LS2-3)

INDEX

Boldface indicates illustrations.

CREDITS

All photos by Emma Wood (emmawoodphotos.co.uk) unless otherwise noted below.

Cover (test tubes background), Barbol/Shutterstock; (girl), KidStock/Blend Images/Getty Images; (fruit salad), margouillat photo/Shutterstock; (splat design), Nicemonkey/Shutterstock; 3 (girl), KidStock/Blend Images/Getty Images; 3 (fruit salad) margouillat photo/Shutterstock; 11 (gum), GrigoryL/Shutterstock; 11 (chocolate), Preto Perola/Shutterstock; 18 (magnet), Mega Pixel/Shutterstock; 18 (cereal), edenexposed/iStockphoto; 23 (jars), design56/Shutterstock; 23 (aluminum foil), cretolamna/Shutterstock; 23 (sock), Evikka/Shutterstock; 26 (top), Pan Xunbin/Shutterstock; 66 (candy), mama_mia/Shutterstock; 76 (insect), GlobalP/iStock

Illustrations by Rachel Fuller.

Thanks to the models: Natasha Chittoo, Tom Johanson, Harry Butler, Alex Paxman, Polly Chamberlain-Webber, Edie Tombleson-Behar, Judah Oyelumade, and Chloe Miller; and to the photo shoot food stylist, Susanna Tee.